a gift for

_____

from

_____

STORIES
ABOUT MOM
from YOUR
FAVORITE
AUTHORS

THE LOVE OF A GODLY MOTHER

COUNTRYMAN®

The loveliest masterpiece

of the heart of God

is the heart of a mother.

THERESE *of* LISIEUX

Every single baby is a brand new

idea from the mind of God.

MAX LUCADO

THE *LOVE* OF A
GODLY MOTHER

MADE WITH LOVE

*I*n my closet hangs a sweater that I seldom wear. It is too small. The sleeves are too short, the shoulders too tight. Some of the buttons are missing, and the thread is frazzled. I should throw that sweater away. I have no use for it. I'll never wear it again. Logic says I should clear out the space and get rid of the sweater.

That's what *logic* says.

But *love* won't let me.

Something unique about that sweater makes me keep it. What is unusual about it? For one thing, it has no label. Nowhere on the garment will you find a tag that reads, "Made in Taiwan." . . . It isn't the product of a nameless employee earning a living. It's the creation of a devoted mother expressing her love.

That sweater is unique. One of a kind. It can't be replaced. Each strand was chosen with care. Each thread was selected with affection.

It is valuable not because of its function, but because of its maker.

MAX LUCADO
THE APPLAUSE OF HEAVEN

Let your father and your mother be glad,

and let her who bore you rejoice.

PROVERBS 23:25 (NKJV)

MY HEART IS KNEELING

Lord, forgive me
that I have so little time to spend on my knees.
Raising children and running a busy house,
I have to do most of my praying
"on the hoof," as it were.
But, Lord, You know my heart is kneeling.

RUTH BELL GRAHAM
PRAYER'S FROM A MOTHER'S HEART

THE WAY TO BE RICH

My mother believed to her dying day that it was a sad woman indeed who didn't have a young child somewhere in her life. She also felt there was no excuse for *not* having one. If you didn't have one handy, you could *get* one—in Sunday school, in a church nursery, a pintsize human who lives down the street—all the while, relieving a young mom and adding something worth more than a hill of beans to your life. She'd tell you that you could find a child almost anywhere you find a lot of *life*. But find one indeed. Because to her you would be a miserable soul if you lost touch with children. I am deeply indebted to my mother for teaching me that one way to be rich was to be rich in children. And, thank goodness, they don't all have to be your own.

BETH MOORE

FEATHERS FROM MY NEST

THE HAND OF GOD

Once many years ago when I was going through a dark period I prayed and prayed, but the heavens seemed to be brass. I felt as though God had disappeared and that I was alone with my trial and burden. It was a dark night for my soul.

I wrote my mother about the experience and will never forget her reply: "Son, there are many times when God withdraws to test your faith. He wants you to trust Him in the darkness. Now, Son, reach up by faith in the fog and you will find that His hand will be

there." In tears I knelt by my bed and experienced an overwhelming sense of God's presence.

BILLY GRAHAM

HOPE FOR EACH DAY

A House Filled with Music

Being part of a musical family was one of God's greatest gifts to our household, not to mention my own soul. As children, we used to gang around the piano before bedtime and sing together. Mother would play piano and all of us (except Daddy, who played harmonica) harmonized to campfire songs, hymns we had memorized, or little ditties that were popular during the early forties. I well remember doing that for an hour or so, then as we were getting ready for bed, the phone would ring.

"Hi. This is Mrs. Bloodworth next door. Please don't stop singing; you're lulling my kids to sleep."

My mother would laugh and explain that her own kids needed to sleep, too, feeling proud of her musical brood. Life in the Swindoll household always included music. . . . A home without music is poorer than the one without money.

LUCI SWINDOLL
I MARRIED ADVENTURE

THE HALLMARK OF MOTHER'S LIFE

As a teenager growing up, my room in our house was directly over Mother's. At night I could see the lights from her room reflected on the trees outside my window. When I slipped downstairs hoping to talk to her a few minutes, I would find her shapely form bent beside her bed in prayer. It was useless to wait for her to rise because she would be there for hours on end, so I would trudge back up to my room. And no matter how early

I awoke in the morning, I would see those lights from her window once again reflected on the trees outside. When I tumbled down the stairs, I would find her seated at her big, flat-top desk, earnestly studying one of the fourteen different translations of the Bible spread out around her. My mother chose to make abiding in Christ one of the priorities of her life.

Mother's abiding is rooted in a love relationship with Jesus that is the secret of her life. As a result of her abiding, and the obedience that is integrated into it, the hallmark of Mother's life is joy. Her face radiates it! Her eyes sparkle with it!

ANNE GRAHAM LOTZ
MY HEART'S CRY

Unto us a Child is born, unto us a Son is given;

and the government will be upon His shoulder.

And His name will be called Wonderful,

Counselor, Mighty God, Everlasting

Father, Prince of Peace.

ISAIAH 9:6 (NKJV)

I am thanking God that unto us a Child was born. I am thanking Him that there was a pure-hearted woman prepared to receive that Child with all that motherhood would mean of daily trust, daily dependence, daily obedience.

ELIZABETH ELLIOT

THE POWERFUL ROLE OF A MOTHER

There is no more influential or powerful role on earth than a mother's. Significant as political, military, education, or religious public figures may be, none can compare to the impact made by mothers. Their words are never fully forgotten, their touch leaves an indelible impression, and the memory of their presence lasts a lifetime. . . .

Abraham Lincoln was right: "No one is poor who had a godly mother." Instead of camping on the negatives and emphasizing how far many mothers have drifted from this magnificent calling to shape the future of our country, I want to throw out a positive challenge. Ladies, this is your hour . . . your distinct opportunity to soar! A harmonious marital partnership and a solid, unselfish commitment to motherhood have never been of greater importance to you or, for that matter, to our nation. Talk about a challenge worth your effort! In spite of what you may have heard, this role is the most dignified, the most influential, and the most rewarding in all the world.

CHARLES SWINDOLL

GROWING WISE IN FAMILY LIFE

How Inventive!

My older brother, Don, was a preemie, but unlike today, with our teams of medical specialists and preemie wards to assist newborns, my nervous parents had to take their infant son home to nurture him. Because he was so fragile, my mom swaddled him and tucked him inside a boot box on a pint-sized pillow. That way she could take care of her household chores and still have him within eyeshot, as she and the box moved from room to room. I guess that was Mom's version of a portable crib.

On cold winter days, Mom heated the oven and left the oven door ajar to warm the kitchen so her precious cargo in the boot box, propped on a nearby chair, would stay toasty warm.

Imagine tucking the first fruit of your womb inside a shoe box. How inventive!

PATSY CLAIRMONT

THE SHOE BOX

MOTHER SHOWED ME JESUS

My first impression of Jesus was my mother. I could have sung this song, "Jesus loves me, this I know, for my mother shows me so."

Mother never considered it a sacrifice to stay home with us children. We were all full of life and quite a handful; however, though she never complained, I think at times that it must have been difficult. Knowing that her husband was traveling the world, meeting interesting people, seeing exciting places, and doing what many considered a great work for the Lord, she must have now and then felt "confined" to the mountains of North Carolina, with five small children and all that this entailed. I never realized just how hard this must have been until I had my seven.

Mother has often been asked how she raised us with Daddy being gone so much of the time. Her immediate reply has always been, "On my knees."

GIGI GRAHAM
A QUIET KNOWING

HELPLESS LAUGHTER

During my growing up years, almost every evening was spent with the sound of my mother's well-modulated voice reading aloud to my father. Together they read nearly all the classics of literature. The memory of her sitting at the end of the couch next to the lamp while Dad languidly stretched out with his head in her lap fills me with soft peace.

Mom's gentle seriousness, coupled with her genuine appreciation of Dad's and my unpredictable humor, was a wonderful balance for me as I grew up. I realized not every-one is inherently quirky and not everyone sees the funny side of life first. But I also learned that everyone has the capacity to develop an

appreciation for the quirky. I saw it every time Mom's mouth began to work in that special way of hers that always culminated in helpless laughter.

MARILYN MEBERG
I'D RATHER BE LAUGHING

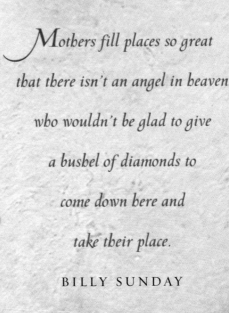

Mothers fill places so great

that there isn't an angel in heaven

who wouldn't be glad to give

a bushel of diamonds to

come down here and

take their place.

BILLY SUNDAY

"YOU CAN'T BE AROUND MAMA AND BE SAD"

I once overhead a woman ask my daughter Vikki, "Is your mother happy like this all the time?" She meant did I laugh and seem to enjoy life all the time.

If Vikki were one to roll her eyes, she might have rolled them then. "Yes," she replied with a sigh. "She makes me tired. I can't even have a bad day around her. You know, some days I just want to feel sorry for myself, but you can't be around Mama and be sad for long."

Well, I took that as a compliment! I'm glad she can't have a bad day around me. Why would anybody want to have a bad day anyway?

THELMA WELLS
THE BUZZ

A Lovely, Rich Legacy

"Old age isn't for sissies," the saying goes. As a woman finds her years of living piling up, she can use them to create a self-centered, miserable demeanor or a lovely, rich legacy of wisdom and wonder to pass on to other women in process.

I never knew my grandmothers. So the treasures of wisdom passed down to me in my family have come primarily from my mother and her sisters.

What a grand bunch of women they are: positive, kind, caring, and fun.

When I consider the legacy that has been passed on to me, I think, *I had better not start to whine. Mother and the aunties will be on me like white on rice.* They have given me priceless gifts. What a privilege I've had to rub shoulders with women like these.

JAN SILVIOUS
BIG GIRLS DON'T WHINE

MUM'S FAITH KEPT US STRONG

My dad died when I was four years old. Left with three children under the age of seven, my mum's prayer was, "God, I pray You will spare me to see Frances, Sheila, and Stephen grow up to love and trust You. That's all I ask."

There was never enough money to pay the bills, but Mum managed somehow. She was careful with every penny, and members of the church we attended would help from time to time. Mum was an incredible inspiration to us all. She believed God would provide what we needed, and she prayed for those needs with simple faith. She never got bitter or angry with God over her lot. She was like a rock for our

family, and her faith kept us strong. She knew that God is faithful.

SHEILA WALSH

LIFE IS TOUGH BUT GOD IS FAITHFUL

THE TOMBOY IN THE TUTU

My mother enrolled me in ballet class. She would drag me off the ball field, put me in the car, and talk excitedly about the recital at the end of the year. (What excited me about it was that the recital meant the end of dance lessons until the fall.) Every week I arrived with a stomachache. I saw sweet little girls and sweet little outfits. And *I* was—the tomboy in the tutu.

My mother finally came to her senses when her

greatly anticipated recital night came along. She invited some of our relatives including my grandma Troccoli. Because I never practiced, I never learned the dance routine. I was about to be handed over to the lions.

The curtain opened. There I was, paralyzed, a human mannequin. *What could I do to prove I was real?* I started shuffling my feet. In years to come my mother would recall the remark from Grandma Troccoli that became my salvation:

"Whatsa matta witha Katalena?"

My mother knew then and there that her dream was my nightmare. Praise God from whom all blessings flow!

KATHY TROCCOLI

THE COLORS OF HIS LOVE

MOTHER TAUGHT ME TO PRAY

*I*n one of my earliest memories, I am seated close to my mother at the foot of my bed. My toes squirm into the lushness of purple shag carpeting. My restless fingers trace the rickrack trim on the Sunbonnet Sue quilt sewn by my great-grandmother. Phrase by phrase, mother speaks the words to the Lord's Prayer. Phrase by phrase, I repeat them back to her. "Our Father, which art in heaven. . . ."

CHRISTA KINDE

DISCOVERING GOD'S WILL FOR YOUR LIFE

THE GIFT OF ADAPTATION

Along with Scripture verses, choruses, manners, and the proper dress code, the greatest thing my mother passed on to us was the gift of adaptation. I am almost certain that my mother invented the phrase "When life gives you lemons. . . ." Mom and Dad instilled in us not only the joy of a good glass of lemonade but also the thrill of making it yourself!

We never considered ourselves well-off financially.

We seldom considered ourselves poor. We simply didn't consider ourselves. My wardrobe was filled with hand-me-downs and homemade dresses my grandmother would send us every fall for the upcoming school year. When we wore shoes, they were usually  tennis shoes or sandals. Since we lived in the South, barefoot was vogue!

CHONDA PIERCE
SECOND ROW, PIANO SIDE

THE JOY AND THE LOVE

*B*abies can be fabulous—and lots of fun. A baby is a small member of the family who can make the love stronger, the days shorter, the nights longer, and the bankroll smaller. When a baby is born, the home will be happier—even if the clothes are shabbier. . . . When more babies come along, the work is multiplied, that's true—but so are the joy and the love.

BARBARA JOHNSON
LEAKING LAFFS

I Like Children

I like the way they're always full of surprises . . . how they have a mind of their own from the very beginning. . . .

I like the way they come to your hospital room in a plain white blanket, wrapped so tightly and with such precision you wonder if they'll have to wear it to college.

I like how they look in their baby bed the very first time you tuck them in it—so small you decide they better sleep in your room.

I like the funny expressions they make while they're dozing and how they crack an awkward smile as if they've tagged an angel.

I like the way they yawn with their whole bodies.

I like the way they love you more than anyone else on earth has ever loved you.

I like the first time they reach their arms out to you.

I like having the prerogative not to lay them down for a nap and rocking them instead for all three hours if you have a mind to.

I like how little girls think pink chiffon dresses are divine and little boys wear their cowboy boots with shorts.

I like the way little girls prefer umbrellas and little boys—puddles.

I like how your children like you even better when they're grown. And how, if you're really lucky, they might have children of their own. And you can try it once more.

BETH MOORE

THINGS PONDERED

What a peace is ours

when we realize God Himself

has promised to carry the respon-

sibility for our children!

They were His before

they became ours.

He will be their teacher.

He will establish them in

righteousness and peace.

PAULA RINEHART

A Faithful Mother

My mother-in-law, who is now a resident of heaven, was used only once, as far as she knew, to lead someone to Christ. That seven-year-old boy was just an ordinary little boy, and no one could know that forty years later Stuart Briscoe would be used throughout the world to lead many, many people to Christ.

JILL BRISCOE
HERE AM I LORD . . .

MOTHER'S PRAYERS FOR ME

My eyes fell upon an old work by a British pastor of yesteryear, F. B. Meyer. It was not his words that spoke to me that evening, however, but the words of my mother. For as I began looking through it, I realized the book had once been a part of her library; after her death in 1971 it had found its way into mine. In her inimitable handwriting, my mother had added her own observations and prayers. Inside the back cover she had written: "Finishing reading this, May 8, 1958."

When I saw that date . . . 1958 . . . memory carried me back to a tiny island in the South Pacific where I had spent many lonely months as a Marine. There, in May of '58, I had reached a crossroad in my own spiritual pilgrimage. In fact, I had entered these words in my own journal at the time: "The Lord has convinced me that I am to be in His service. I need to begin my plans to prepare for a lifetime of ministry."

As I scanned Mother's words, I found one reference after another to her prayers for me as I was far away . . . her concern for my spiritual welfare . . . her desire for God's best in my life.

CHARLES SWINDOLL
THE FINISHING TOUCH

WATCHING AND
LISTENING TO MOM

Mom, I was listening. And what you taught me has often been a helpful nudge in the right direction. Of course, the most important signposts you left me were the ones directed toward Jesus and His ways. I'm grateful you allowed Him to change your life when you were in your late thirties. Otherwise, you could have been a taskmaster (me, too)

instead of a tenacious teacher of truth. I watched your life, attitudes, and heart enlarge as you followed the Lord with the same passion and devotion you heaped on your family. . . . Thank you for showing me how simple attitudes and actions can enhance my journey every step of the way.

PATSY CLAIRMONT

THE GREAT ADVENTURE

GOOD ADVICE

Mother told me once when I wanted to give up on a friendship that wasn't going my way to look at it from the other person's point of view. She said something like, "You can't make people into what you want them to be. People are themselves. They're cut out of their own cloth. Try to think about what you can give them, not what they can give you." That was good advice. And she was an example of that to her friends.

We had neighbors all around us who didn't know the Lord, and Mother never stopped doing good, listening to their troubles, or giving love to them in Jesus' name. When Thelma Roberts, a neighbor and close friend, was widowed and had no children to step in, Mother cared for her the remainder of her life. . . .

Thelma told me shortly before she passed away that my mother had saved her life. "She reached out to me when I had nobody else. She just never stopped giving, and she never asked anything of me. I owe her my life. What a friend!"

LUCI SWINDOLL
I MARRIED ADVENTURE

MOMS ARE A BREED APART

Only a mother can powder a baby's behind with one hand and hold the phone with the other. Only a mom can discern which teen is entering the door just by the sound of the key in the lock. Only a mom can spend a day wiping noses, laundering enough socks for the Yankees, balancing a checkbook down to $4.27, and still mean it when she thanks God for her kids. Only a mom.

Some things only a mom can fix. Like Hamburger Helper without the hamburger. Like the cabinet door her husband couldn't and his bruised ego when he found out that she could. Broken shoelace? Broken heart? Breaking out on your face? Breaking up with your sweetheart? Moms can handle that. Some things only a mom can fix.

Some things only a mom can know. The time it takes to drive from piano lesson to Little League practice? She knows. How many pizzas you need for a middle school sleepover? Mom knows. . . .

We men usually don't. The kids are usually clueless. Moms are a breed apart.

MAX LUCADO
NEXT DOOR SAVIOR

SING THROUGH THE STORM

At a time of unanswered prayer in my life years ago, my mother taught me the verse to a hymn that I still quote when I am totally baffled by events that seem to careen out of the orbit of what I have asked:

Trust Him when dark doubts assail thee,
Trust Him when thy strength is small,
Trust Him when to simply trust Him,
Seems the hardest thing of all.

ANNE GRAHAM LOTZ
MY HEART'S CRY

MOM THE BRICKLAYER!

From where we sat, we could see just about everything going on in church. We had a good view of Mom, who was playing the piano. In fact, we were close enough that we could discern just the lightest lifting of her brow, the sort of movement that told us all to be very, very still—or else. . . .

Mom was . . . our drama coach, our piano teacher, our own live-in Emily Post. . . . Somewhere during the course of all the talent contests, Scripture memorization, recitals, and essay writings, a belief system was born. A single stone was laid. When I believed my mother to be laboring in the fields of arts and crafts by sewing costumes for Christmas plays, writing poems for special Sunday night services, sounding out the hard-to-read names from the Bible so that I could understand them, she was actually working as a stonemason, laying the solid, intricate teachings that would someday form a foundation.

Mom the bricklayer! There were no stories of babies who came from cabbage patches—babies came from Jesus. . . . There were no ridiculous theories that we evolved from some huge explosion in the sky—God put us here. Mother told us about the gospel. She read it to us. We memorized it. We believed it.

CHONDA PIERCE
SECOND ROW, PIANO SIDE

OVER THE RAINBOW

I had no idea it would be this wonderful! Sure, I had watched my sister care for her sons and saw her joy at every little step they took. But I had no idea having my own child would be like landing over the rainbow and waking up in Oz.

I also had no idea my body could be stretched to those proportions without bursting or that my heart could either. I've noticed too that in the few moments of sleep you get when your children are babies, God mysteriously and wondrously tucks love into your heart. You find your ocean of love is so deep it can carry you across the rough water of sleeplessness.

SHEILA WALSH

WE BRAKE FOR JOY

NOW MOTHER CAN LAUGH

Eleven or twelve hours following my mom's death I was in the shower, which often serves as my sanctuary, and was thinking about her. I tried to internalize the enormity of what had happened that day. She was at that very moment in heaven. What did she feel? What was it like? She was actually in the presence of God! I tried to visualize her in her new surroundings; as I did, I became lost to my own. A vision of my mother began to appear on the screen of my mind. I saw her in the arms of Jesus. He was holding her as one would a child, cradling her against His body. Her face was radiant and as Jesus held her, He began to gently swing her back and forth in His arms. Back and forth—back and forth—and she began to laugh and laugh, until her head was thrown back in total abandonment. At first I was a bit startled by this image of my mother, but as joy and relief flooded over me I thought, *Well, of course. She can laugh now. . . . God has wiped away all her tears and now she can laugh again . . . and again . . . and again.*

MARILYN MEBERG

CHOOSING THE AMUSING

A SPECIAL ANGEL

Up in heaven a child was ready to be born. The child asked God, "I know You are sending me to earth tomorrow, but how can I survive there? I am so small and helpless."

God replied, "I have chosen a special angel for you there. She will love you and take care of you."

"Here in heaven, Lord, I don't do anything but sing and smile. What will I do on Earth? I won't know how to sing the songs down there."

"Your angel will sing for you," God replied, "and she'll teach you how to sing, too. And you'll learn to laugh as well as smile. Your angel and I will take care of that."

"But how will I understand what people say to me? I don't know a single word of the language they speak!"

"Your angel will say the sweetest things you will ever hear, and she will teach you, word by word, how to speak the language."

"And when I want to talk to You. . . ?"

"Your angel will gently place your little hands together and teach you how. That's the simplest language of all. It's called prayer."

"Who will protect me there, God?"

"Your angel is soft and gentle, but if something threatens you, there is no stronger force on Earth than the power she'll use to defend you."

"I'll be sad not getting to see You anymore."

"I will always be next to you, even though you can't see Me. And your angel will teach you the way to come back to Me if you stray."

Then it was time to go. Excited voices could be heard from earth, anticipating the child's arrival. In a hurry, the babe asked softly, "Oh God, if I must go now, please tell me my angel's name!"

And God replied, "You will call your angel . . . *Mommy*."

SOURCE UNKNOWN

MOTHER MODELED CHRIST

*I*t was a privilege to grow up surrounded by my mother's friends. Because she had eight children she didn't go to places to visit. Her friends came to her, and I listened to their conversations.

Those wonderful women modeled a caring Christ-like community. When anyone was sick or in trouble, or when there was a death in the family, my mother and

her friends rallied to
provide whatever was
needed: a meal, a helping
hand, a listening ear.
They were a blessing
in one another's lives.
They demonstrated love,

which through the years increased. Even today their
influence shapes me.

MARY GRAHAM

WOMEN OF FAITH DEVOTIONAL BIBLE

MOM AND GOD'S PROMISES

I was born with a pulmonary defect which weakened the muscles around my heart. As my condition worsened, my mother was told that I would die before I started school. But one day, as a new Christian reading her Bible, Mom realized this news was contrary to Scripture she'd read such as, "My people shall never be put to shame" (Joel 2:26 NKJV). Mom decided to "spend" God's promises, and she went out and bought my school clothes and enrolled me in kindergarten.

Mom's faith was tested often as I continued to miss many days of school that year. At some point, however, things turned around, and I grew stronger. By the end of first grade, I had won a physical fitness award. In the years to come, free from all heart problems, I became the biggest tomboy in my family.

"My people shall never be put to shame." That meant my mom, and that means you and me.

LYNDA HUNTER-BJORKLUND
WOMEN of FAITH DEVOTIONAL BIBLE

MOTHER'S FERVENT PRAYERS

One of my favorite remembrances of Mom is of the days I'd walk into a room and see her with her Bible spread out in her lap searching the Scriptures. I now have her Bible, but I don't use it because she wore it out. It's a loose pile of pages with a detached, tattered leather cover that has a golden sketch of Christ shepherding sheep on it.

Mom knew about sheep, especially straying ones. My brother, sister, and I all had extended seasons of rebellion toward her and the Lord. We thought she had too many rules and her standards were too high for us to attain. And each of us believed we could handle life without the help of her God. We were wrong. I'm grateful that the Lord heard our mother's fervent prayers, and He had mercy on us. Each of us eventually gave our sin-sick hearts to the Lord Jesus, and we thanked Him that He and our mom never gave up on us. Hope keeps a mother's light glowing.

PATSY CLAIRMONT

I GREW UP LITTLE

MY STORYTELLING MOTHER

I had a storytelling mother. I usually heard them at bedtime. . . . My mother was good with words; she was also good with *tones*. In her storytelling I not only saw whole worlds come into being, I felt them within me through the timbre of her voice.

She told stories of her parents, who had brought eleven children from Norway to the sparsely populated but promised land of Montana to begin a new life. Mostly, though, she told Bible stories. And among Bible stories, the David stories took pride of place—not to the exclusion of Moses and Elijah and Jesus. . . .

When I was older and reading the Bible for myself, I was surprised, but also a little disappointed, to find that some of the details that I loved most were extracanonical. She didn't scruple, I realized, to considerably improve the biblical version when she felt like it. But I also realized, in my adult assessment of her narrative practice, that she rarely, if ever, violated or distorted the story itself. She held the entire Story, from Genesis to Revelation, in her believing imagination, with Jesus as the central and controlling presence throughout. However many details she got wrong (or invented), she never got the Story wrong—she knew it inside and out, knew  Jesus obediently, the Holy Spirit reliving these texts in her as she prayed her way through the years in our Montana valley.

EUGENE H. PETERSON

LEAP OVER A WALL

OUR CHILDREN BELONG TO GOD

*I*n the first chapter of 1 Samuel we can read the story of Hannah, who longed for a son more than any thing else in the world. Her husband did not understand the depth of her pain, and his second (fertile) wife taunted her. But Hannah persisted in asking God for a son and made Him a vow:

She made a vow and said, *"O LORD of hosts, if You will indeed look on the affliction of Your maidservant and*

remember me, and not forget Your maidservant, but will give Your maidservant a male child, then I will give him to the LORD all the days of his life. . . ."
(1 Samuel 1:11, NKJV)

Within a year she gave birth to Samuel. She cradled him in her arms and remembered her vow. Now I don't know about you, but it's hard to imagine wanting a baby as badly as Hannah did and then knowing she would have to give him up one day soon! But she took him to live with

Eli the priest. She knew that Samuel did not come into this world for her, but for God. He belonged to the Lord. She gave Samuel back to Him. . . .

God took care of Samuel, and He blessed Hannah with three more sons and two daughters! Samuel grew to be a judge of Israel, a prophet, and a priest. I know plenty of young moms who worry about sending their children out into the world, but that is what God asks us to do, isn't it?

JAN SILVIOUS
BIG GIRLS DON'T WHINE

A LITTLE PRAYER BOOK

My mother encouraged me as a little girl to pray specifically. She bought me a small white leather notebook, and in it I carefully recorded my requests. Then, at her instruction, I left a blank line under each one so I could record the date of the answer. In the front of the little book, she penned these words:

Thou art coming to a King,
Large petitions with thee bring,
For His grace and power are such,
None can ever ask too much!

ANNE GRAHAM LOTZ
MY HEART'S CRY

Remembering Mother

Some of my sweetest memories of my mother center on fragrances. Her thick, wavy, blond hair smelled of Breck shampoo while she sashayed around leaving To a Wild Rose scent in her path. Our home was fragrant too, as she aired the house regularly, scrubbed the interior with pine cleaners, and used big, fat wick deodorizers throughout the rooms.

A fragrant memory I treasure is of my mom hanging

clothes on the line to absorb the outdoor freshness. Her little frame clothed in a tidy shirtwaist dress, stretched to reach the clotheslines. Wooden clothespins filled her apron pockets while a few were clamped between her teeth.

But I think the best smell was Mom's cooking. Nobody, I mean nobody, could beat her Southern fried chicken, baking powder biscuits, gravy, and banana pudding.

PATSY CLAIRMONT

I GREW UP LITTLE

You wove me in my mother's womb.

I will give thanks to You,

for I am fearfully and

wonderfully made.

PSALM 139:13–14 (NASB)

BELIEVING, PRAYING, AND GIVING

Mother used to sing all the time around the house—praise music, hymns, and patriotic songs. I recall one hymn in particular that was often on Mother's lips, "O Zion, Haste." Mother knew all three verses by heart, but it's the third that brings her most vividly to mind:

Give of thy sons to bear the message glorious;
Give of thy wealth to speed them on their way;
Pour out thy soul for them in prayer victorious;
And all thy spending Jesus will repay.

That is exactly what my mother did. She poured out her soul in prayer for her children, she supported us with her spirit of encouragement, and she gave us back to God to do whatever He wanted with us.

With all three of us now in Christian ministry I cannot help but wonder if this is the way Jesus repaid my mom for her years of believing, praying, and giving.

LUCI SWINDOLL
THE GREAT ADVENTURE

MAKING MEMORIES

*I*t may seem strange to those who've never tried to find a quiet, safe place in the city where a kid can learn how to drive without fighting rush-hour traffic and multi-lane freeways, but my son Tim and I chose a nearby cemetery. It was beautiful and peaceful, and my favorite part was that the speed limit was only fifteen miles per hour! We would drive around the beautiful grounds for a while, then we'd head for In-n-Out where I would recover from the experience while Tim stuffed himself with burgers and fries.

Years have passed since Tim and I slowly wound our way through that beautiful cemetery. Now Tim's grave is right there next to the curving road where we drove together. Recently I was there, standing beside his grave, remembering how we laughed as we rode along that cemetery trail.

While I was reliving those bittersweet memories, I could see a little car wending its way along that same path. In the passenger seat was a young mother, probably about thirty-five, and steering the car I could

see a nervous young boy who must have been about fifteen. As the car was coming closer to where I was standing, I wanted to call out to that mother, "Enjoy your ride with him now, while you can. Make a memory of your experience–and go get a hamburger to celebrate!"

BARBARA JOHNSON

LIVING SOMEWHERE BETWEEN ESTROGEN AND DEATH

ACKNOWLEDGEMENTS

Grateful acknowledgment is made to the following publishers for permission to reprint this copyrighted material.

Briscoe, Jill © *Here am I, Lord, . . . Send Somebody Else*
(Nashville: W Publishing Group, 2004).

Clairmont, Patsy © *The Shoe Box* (Nashville: W. Publishing Group, 2003).

Clairmont, Patsy © *I Grew Up Little* (Nashville: W. Publishing Group, 2004).

Graham, Gigi © *A Quiet Knowing* (Nashville: W Publishing Group, 2001).

Graham, Ruth Bell © *Prayer's From a Mother's Heart*
(Nashville: Thomas Nelson, Inc., 1999).

Johnson, Barbara © *Living Somewhere Between Estrogen and Death*
(Nashville: W. Publishing Group, 1997).

Johnson, Barbara © *Leaking Laffs Between Pampers and Depends*
(Nashville: W. Publishing Group, 2000).

Lotz, Anne Graham © *My Heart's Cry* (Nashville: W Publishing Group, 2002).

Lucado, Max © *The Applause of Heaven* (Nashville: W Publishing Group, 1990).

Lucado, Max © *Next Door Savior* (Nashville: W. Publishing Group, 2003).

Meberg, Marilyn© *I'd Rather Be Laughing* (Nashville: W. Publishing Group, 1998).

Meberg, Marilyn© *Choosing the Amusing* (Nashville: W. Publishing Group, 1999).

Moore, Beth © *Things Pondered: From the Heart of a Lesser Woman*
(Nashville: Broadman & Holman, Publishers, 1997).

Moore, Beth ©. *Feathers from My Nest: A Mother's Reflections*
(Nashville: Broadman & Holman, Publishers, 2004).

Peterson, Eugene H. ©. *Leap Over a Wall* (New York: HarperCollins, 1997).

Pierce, Chonda. *Second Row, Piano Side* (Kansas City: Beacon Hill Press©, 1996).

Silvious, Jan ©, *Big Girls Don't Whine* (Nashville: W. Publishing Group, 2003).

Swindoll, Charles ©. *Growing Wise in Family Life*
(Sisters, Oregon: Multnomah Publishers, 1988).

Swindoll, Charles ©. *The Finishing Touch* (Nashville: W Publishing Group, 1994).

Swindoll, Luci ©, *I Married Adventure* (Nashville: W. Publishing Group, 2002).

Walsh, Sheila ©. *Life Is Tough but God Is Faithful*
(Nashville: Thomas Nelson, Inc., 1999).

Wells, Thelma ©. *The Buzz: Seven Power-Packed Scriptures to Energize Your Life*
(Nashville: W Publishing Group, 2004).

Troccoli, Kathy. *The Colors of His Love* (Nashville: W Publishing Group, 2002).

Women of Faith ©. *We Brake for Joy: 90 Devotions to Add Laughter, Fun, and
Faith to Your Life* (Grand Rapids: Zondervan Publishing House, 1998)

Women of Faith ©, *The Great Adventure: A Devotional Journey of the Heart, Soul, and
Mind* (Nashville: W. Publishing Group, 2002).

Women of Faith Devotional Bible (Nashville: Thomas Nelson, Inc., © 2003).

To order additional copies
Call 1-800-933-9673
Or visit
www.nelsonministryservices.com